Title

Raising Teenagers:

The Best Way

Sub Title:

Parents And Teenagers

Reading further should improve the knowledge of teenagers and parents, some parents may understand their teenagers, while others are still trying to find easy steps to communicate on a daily basis.

It is not an easy task to let go of your children when they reach their teenage years; it does remind you as a parent, of when you were a teenager, but times have changed. There is much more to deal with now than before from ages 13-19, parents are faced with difficult issues. For a teenager to be able to experience life, but with limitations, is another issue as some want to do more than that. There are many ways of enjoying and being entertained, as a teenager.

No teenager has to do anything to impress a friend, it can be dangerous to an individual's health, like abuse of alcohol, taking drugs, smoking marijuana, or in contact **with other groups** that have bad influences on your child, and, if your child is new to the outside world, this is an option to learn from family and teachers about how to differentiate from right and wrong. A teenager should not do anything they are not comfortable with.

Girls, on the otherhand should not allow themselves to be degraded by boys, they should respect each other, so it makes it easier for both genders.

Parents have an important part in their children's lives in teaching them to respect others, to trust, to be polite, to be honest, and on how to gain trust: after all, it begins at home. not at your first day of nursery school, preschool, or primary school, the discipline of children should start at an early age with their parents.

It is of great importance to know where your child is out for the night, or at any other time, **(if not at school).** Parents should show interest in their child's day- to- day schedule. Too many boundaries, may only encourage your teenager to do what is not allowed. Every individual thinks differently, so don't compare your teenager with others. Each child understands and sees life in their **own** way.

Language Development

To improve the language of a teenager, reading is a great idea; this allows them to speak properly, and, not to often fall into the slang language. Sometimes, proper use of English words are easily forgotten, in this way.

Personality And Moral Responsibility

A good sense of humour shows personality, smiling at others, whenever you can, friendliness, confidence, able to speak out to people, not being shy, to be more outspoken. When in the classroom interacting with others, you should be able to speak freely. Parents, should ensure that their children, are to be responsible, by setting chores on a daily basis. Having a pet, **joining** the local library, and being punctual when returning borrowed books. Babysitting a neighbour's infant, that shows responsibility too.

Oneself

Physical Maturing

This is a kind of emotional growth to come to terms with oneself, and to allow acceptance. Children, especially, girls in this way, are aware of the changes in their bodies, their sexuality, changes of hormones, breast development, and mood swings, these are the important facts for teenage girls to know, when growing up.

When Does Their Menstruation Cycle Begin?

For some at the age of 11, and for others when older. It is not the same for every girl to be wearing a bra at the same time. Parents, should show an interest, in their teenage girls, and, explain the facts of life, by not feeling embarrassed in using the appropriate words as an explanation.

Family Relationships

Communication between immediate families and extended families like aunts, uncles, grandparents,nieces and nephews, allows teenagers to learn more about themselves. Teenagers learn more about their history from their extended families, like place of birth, their ancestors, and, of understanding each other.

Making Friends

As **teenagers** meet other people, they should learn of their **friends' identity**, the place of birth, friends' background, and, to enable good friendship, and know the person one is acquainted with. It is difficult to trust every one you know, so in this way you learn to trust and be safe. Having friends is important, it allows you to find yourself and have a social life.

How to Meet People

Meeting Other People Can Be Hard In Some Situations, But With Simple Ways, It Can Be Possible

Well, it is in most cases, that you are shy about meeting other people in your community, or if you are in a new school.
Don't be unsure of your thoughts.
Be the first to say hello, greet someone, be jovial. Introduce yourself, and, take it from there, it would either go your way, or maybe it won't; it is something you should take a chance on, at least you know that you have tried, and, will be familiar about your mistakes for what to do next, if you don't succeed.

To meet people, you got to get out there and be positive.

Use your sense of humour, don't try to be something you are not, this will ruin the friendship.

Try have new ideas when with people, remember people's names, ask, if you don't recall, this will make it easy on you to speak up.

Show interest in other people's conversations, and be enthusiastic about issues.

Keep in touch, exchange telephone numbers, meet up, when you want to, and, be punctual.

Encouragement is important, show involvement in previous conversations, too.

Try not to hang on a friend or person in the group. Be independent, respect each other.

Don't show off clothing or jewellery, just be simple.

Interacting with Others

How Do You Communicate?
Are You Confident In Public Places?
Are You A Positive Person?
Do You Feel Comfortable When You Are With Other People?
Are You Free To Make Conversation?

These are just some of the questions, asked by teenagers, parents should communicate with their children about these issues and listen carefully to what is required. Teenagers learn to be confident , to speak and, to be positive with others from their parents and family.

Importance of Teenage Education

It is of great importance for parent, and child to be educated in the new world, there are far too many changes and parents should show their children how to cope with their surroundings. Teenage education is crucial, because there are many challenges to face up to, and with control, it can be possible.

Organisation

Teenagers who read books, should be able to understand the concepts and facts of the information on a specific topic. Books should be on a teenage level, in some cases, it depends on how the concept and information given is grasped by the individual. If a teenager finds it difficult to comprehend, a friend, a parent or the teacher can help solve the problem.

Self Esteem

How Often Do You Lack Self Esteem?

Pessimist and a optimist. Some of us are both, we tend to feel that way when something goes wrong. Love yourself, and be yourself, it makes you feel good, positive, and happy. Try to be more of an optimist, look on the good side of life. This encourages you to be more of a better person. A dull person, looks on the negative side of life, and becomes sad and depressed, a person that never sees anything good which plainly looks at life with a weak attitude, and, thus makes him/her a pessimist.

Relationships, Love, and, Intimacy

How Do You Learn From Relationships, Love, And Intimacy?

Teenagers could learn of a relationship, if they have formed one, you can either be serious about your partner, or it could be an experience for both partners, this could be a learning point and lessons are learned from this relationship. In some cases, you become intimate, as you want to have fun and experience what you need to know about life as a teenager. To know what love feels like, and to create something new.

If your relationship is not going well, take some time to think about it, make a break from it, do not feel you would hurt the opposite sex and is afraid to let go.

One should be able to learn to feel pain too, it makes you a stronger person. All it takes is time to learn, no matter what you decide, it works out for the best. When you make decisions, feel free to go with the flow.

You could only learn from your mistakes, nobody is perfect. Be with friends and family after a break up. It makes you feel better and lets you know that you are still loved. Being alone makes you a vulnerable person. Learn to love someone, when you know you are ready for it, and, then think about trusting the person close to you before trying to be intimately involved.

Why Do Parents Need To Be Educated In Raising Teenagers?

Not many parents are aware of the ways of raising teenagers, this information can be of worth your while. Parents shouldn't yell at their teens, it makes teenagers feel they are not loved by their parents, and become isolated persons, they start seeking friends that feel the same way and turn into the wrong direction. Teenagers, who are lonely and depressed and feel unloved by their parents become street kids or gangsters.

Parent and child fail to understand each other by yelling. By talking to each other, it makes the problem easier, and nobody feels hurt or neglected. Try to do chores around the house and spend quality time together.

Teenagers can only learn at first from their parents, then teachers, other informative books, friends, and extended families. If you are not taught at home, discipline will not be taught on the street, in which case it doesn't go the way you expected, parents should teach discipline at a young age. As their teenagers get older they would grow to be a pleasant and an obedient beings. Not every teenager is the same.

Ways To Be Happy And Stress-Free

When a teenager feels stressed after a day at school or by a family or friend, try to go for a walk. Get some sunshine, have a full 8 hours of sleep. Play with your pet, if you have one. Be happy, have a smile, to feel good, it doesn't cost you much to be this way.

Try not to bother about bickering, outdoor activities make your mind feel relaxed. Call a friend, go out for coffee, be nice to people, talk to your neighbours, **just be yourself**. Have a day out, have a bus ride into town, visit the shopping mall, you don't have to go shopping to feel good either.

Get involved with a **fund -raising** event, or an organisation, where you are able to help others and also, it would make them feel good. Make the most of your valuable time, enjoy each day.

By spending more time outdoors, especially, if the weather is good you will feel good. If you are happy from the inside of you, then it will show on your face. A clear proof of how you feel. Sunshine is good for you, for ten to fifteen minutes a day, as it boosts your immune system, just a tip.

If you have problem sleeping, inhale, deep breathing, hold it for ten seconds, and then breathe out, do this a few times, you will be able to relax and fall asleep.

Dressing: How Should Teenagers Dress?

Well, that depends on the individual as a teenager. How you dress represents you, in public, but not every teenager wants to be a sloppy dresser. Some teens dress according to fashion, and others wear what they like or can afford to buy. Advice from the concerned parent, helps to make amends when it comes to ideas of dressing a teenager. Try to dress appropriately for the occasion, use make-up lightly, with guidance. Parents should be aware of their children's ideas, and, in sharing their opinions together.

Mothers and daughters, should plan shopping together, to buy what is affordable and having to talk about any issues in the process. When your son has reached his teenage years, he would feel most comfortable discussing his ideas with dad.

Dating

When Should A Teenager Start Dating?

Dating starts when teenagers feel they are ready to experience one of the most exciting part of their lives. When dating, they shouldn't feel shy, hangout with friends in your own age group, you will notice that you will have lots in common. Do not use fake identities because your friends do. Respect each others' wishes. When friends get together to go out for parties, make sure they are easily contactable.

The party should be in a safe environment, when you feel like leaving the party call a taxi, a trusted friend or family. Never get into a car with a drunk driver. It can be dangerous for both of you. Always wait with a friend in a lit up area for your transport, if it is delayed. Let your parents know of your whereabouts. Parents should trust their children; this will prevent their teenagers from telling lies.

How To Break Up

To Be Free From An Unhappy Relationship

To be in a long- term relationship, is an experience for partners. When you are in love with someone, it becomes an ache of love, which is supposed to be a good feeling. If you feel pain when in love, then, this eventually makes you an unhappy person in a relationship.

You would want to be free from this relationship, if you are unhappy, breaking up with someone is hard to deal with, but this is to make your lives less complicated, and to go further with new experiences.

When you have made the decision, to break up, bear in mind, that, your reason must be a good one. To be able to do so, remember to be polite and private about it.

Don't be friends after the break up, the relationship should be over, and keep it that way. You can't be enemies either, but, if you keep in touch, you will end up right where you first started, making the same mistakes and falling into the same old habits. This will make you miserable. Something, that, you wouldn't want to do.

To accept the break up, is an important issue on both sides. Take sometime out, go away on a short trip, think about meeting different people, feel happy again, become independent and make new friends. Trusting another individual, may not be easy, but at least, there will be time to heal and planning your future, is a great idea. Remember that trust is easily lost and hard to re-gain.

Try not to keep memory cards lying around your room or home of your partner. Photos, greeting cards, letters or notes should be put away in a box and kept out of sight. These little reminders, just adds to the sadness you are experiencing. Don't have negative thoughts, as it makes you depressed, sad, and a distraught person. Be with loved ones at this time.

You will have the feeling of anger, despair and uncertainty, but, talk to friends, and you will feel better. This helps you to cope with pain and feel at ease. It is not the end of the world. Take care of yourself, self-control is very important at this time, try not to neglect yourself in any way. There will always be someone else to make you happy.

One of the issues, in a relationship, is being taken for granted, and this could **cause** bad **communication**. Your break up, could be about something that has been discussed from before, or at numerous times, and, still one of you failed to comply to each other.

Don't give in easily, if the other person tries to change your mind to stay and try again to work things out. Think of the reason you are getting out of this relationship. If you are not satisfied, then you shouldn't be together.

If you don't leave when you should have, then, when in a marriage, your problems will just get bigger. Teenagers shouldn't feel the need of an early commitment in a relationship.

A break up should be approached, with gentleness, and do it fast, no hesitations or being insecure about your thoughts. In some cases, lashing out, anger, and, crying is expected. Whatever comes to mind is mentioned, and moods are different. Forgive each other and move on.

If you have a good relationship, and feel love, have the understanding and communication, then you may be together. Learn to grow in love, a love like this lasts.

Parent and teenage education, is to allow the parent to teach their teenagers about the facts of life, teenagers require to know not only what is important but, also, how to live as teenagers. Living in a safe environment is very important for your children.

As teenagers, you could be gullible while listening to others, and, befriend someone with a strange character, and, in this way it leads to other problems. If living in a safe area, there may not be doubts in trusting your neighbour, if necessary precautions are taken.

Teach your child, from a young age, that an individual has to work, in order to earn a living, this is important. When your child is a teenager, it is fully understood that in life you have to be independent at some point. An opportunity for your child to experience working, and, appreciate what is earned.
It is not good for both parents, to hand over money to their children, whenever it is required, easy access to money, should not be taken for granted when living with parents. This is what makes teenagers lazy and not to work. They feel that if money comes so easily,

'Why Work?'

As parents, you shouldn't give the wrong impression to teenagers, by buying gifts or presents for every school award or birthday that comes along, it is not a great idea. Financial control must be taught, this is to prevent your children from falling into financial debt as they get older, and raise their own families. Teenagers, should be taught of how to spend money wisely, have a well-planned budget.

If you have a beer pocket, don't live a champagne life, meaning live by what you earn, and can afford. One of the common ways of going into debts, is when you have money and show-off about it to your friends and, don't realise that you have spent more than your monthly budget.
The way parents live is reflected on their children. If parents spend lavishly, then so will their children.

Teenagers should be free to explore. It is not a good idea sitting and watching long hours of television and being by the computer. Allow yourselves a time-table, each day, so you make time for visiting a friend, going for walks, do some interesting outdoor activity, be active in sports, be sociable, be communicative. Ride your bike, go to the park, or have a picnic.

It is good to get to know your neighbours, and be able to relate to one another, in case of an emergency.
Learn more about your environment.

Some parents, have difficulty in raising their teens and some find it easy.

Being a single parent can be difficult when raising a teenager, the authority toward your child is not strong enough, because as single parents, you got to work long hours and still be there for your child; this can be a tiring effort as not much time is spent with your teenage child. In this case it is an idea to arrange with other family members to help you, to avoid problematic issues.

In some cases children get bored, and get involved with the wrong group of children and in the process become the bad one.
Whereas, in a home with both parents it can be easier, teenage children are safe and know authority. The home is family -orientated and both parents can make decisions, if necessary, for their children.

Although teenagers shouldn't be pressured to live as their parents wish them to, guidance from parents, is important, this allows teenagers to know they are capable of living independently.

Educating Teenagers

Parents should try to make time for their children, set a time schedule to have open discussions about dating, and about diseases like **STD**, being contracted when with several different partners, during intercourse. **Sex** discussions are very important.

How Is STD Caused?

What Is AIDS?

About SEX, With Different Partners?

Is It safe To Have Sex With More Than One Partner?

How Safe Is It When Using A Condom?

Avoiding Teenage Pregnancies!!!!

How Often Are You Told That A 17 Year Old Is Pregnant?

By talking to your teenage daughters about life, this kind of issues can be resolved. Mothers should to try to be more open in conversation or discussions. To speak freely of **sex education** it is of great importance, the curfew hour may not help much, to be intimate the hour is not accounted for, this can occur in seconds an intimate act can be uncontrollable. This can be a monument task to talk to your teenager about the facts of life, but, now that it is all over the media, it should be slightly easier. Talk of body sexual organs, the normalcy of feelings, the physical act of sex, the development of understanding, when sex oriented, and how babies are made.

Sex ties to dating, and it can be for a short or a long term relationship. This allows your teenager to be informed, to be aware of the exploitation of sex abuse, and when an individual is allowed sex with consent or when sex is denied.

How Are Your Children Eating? Are Your Children Eating Healthy Foods? Are They Aware Of Eating Disorders, Like Anorexia, Bulimia, And Obesity?

Eating correctly can prevent eating disorders. Professional help, is always available if there is a problem. If parents pay attention to their children they will notice changes of eating disorders.

How Do Teenagers Differentiate-Between Intimate Relationships?

The **gender** differences in a person being gay, a lesbian, and same sex friendship. There is love in relationships of the same sex gender, and the opposite sex. Topics like this should be discussed not to confuse teenagers, and to let them know that not every acquaintance or relationship is the same and to be educated by it.

At the ages from 13-19 are the most important part of a teenager's life, they should be allowed to experience whatever possible and learn about themselves. Life is like a roller coaster ride, only a bit slower.

The adolescent stage, when teenagers feel the need to be with others of the same age group, and to participate in sports, and when teens look for their own interests.

Parents who are, sensitive and responsible have children that grow with assurance to feel safe, secure, and are able to form relationships with the opposite sex easily and trust easily too.

Your Qualities

This is a stage, when your teenager/s should be thinking of having goals to believe in something of a worthy future. To believe in one's self.

What's Their Choice Of Career?

How Are They Going To Pay For Their College Fees?

Setting Goals

This subject shouldn't be overlooked.
Teenagers have a new prospective on life.

Why Should This Subject Be Unexplored?

They have energy at this age, to achieve any goals possible, at times, teens lack the experience to sit and think about their goals, some teenagers, in most cases, have too much to focus on, than to think about their achievements.

When given time, teenagers can work on their achievements, no matter how big or small their goal is, it can be achieved. Modern teenagers face great challenges to achieve what they want out of life, and, have endless choices, by making steady progress in their needs any goal can be achieved. Once teenagers reach the age of 18 they should be able to face responsibility.

Parents should raise teenagers to rely upon on their own mind power, and not follow other parents in doing so. Don't do what other parents imply to their teens, it is not always safe or good for you when parenting.

Teenagers have a wide-open future, and, lots of competition, so they require to be motivated by others close to them, to be encouraged to achieve whatever interests them the most. This allows teenagers to explore freely.

Helping teenagers to think of their own ideas to allow them to achieve their own goals is what a teenager strives for, and if he or she fails in the attempt to achieve what is really desired, don't let your teenager be discouraged. There are always other opportunities.

Show your teenager positivity in future attempts of achievement. To help a teenager to be focused on their achievements, they've got to look at what it is, they really want out of life at this point.

Teenagers should explore what is in front of them, to emphasise on their talents and desires. Friends help each other to create new ideas, to be able to communicate, and, guide those who are interested in setting goals.

Learning to be with new people, and the value of friendship is a teenagers' desire. To be able to help others in need share alike, don't be rude to other people. Serve your community, makes you a better person by doing something to improve lives of other people like the homeless, help the blind, the deaf or the handicapped – **volunteering.**

Trusting and knowing your child will make it easier on parents because it can be difficult to let your child go free when you have spent your whole life caring, and now it is time to let go. Believe in your child, only, you the parent could know your child better than others do. Love your children equally, but not differently, this weakens your child's strength in thought and affects children in both, childhood, and adulthood.

It should be the same in trusting your children. One **should'nt** be over-protective when it comes to raising teenage children, life for teenagers are different. There are more choices to explore.

Achieving goals, is an exciting task for a teenager, this allows them to look forward, to be able to accomplish what they want. Their choice of university, career, to get that diploma, to work part-time during the summer holidays, to get their driver's licence, and have driving privileges and goals can be achieved by motivation. Summer holidays, it is an exciting time of the year, looking for fun, they want to find themselves.

They can work on summer holidays to pay part of their college fees with the help of their parents, if planned that way. If your child shows interest in further studying there should be no doubt about helping with the payment.

Who are they?

What are they capable of?

Time of experiment, they want to be older and to belong in society, and to be in an age group they find interesting and enjoyable. The number of teens in the world is growing and will continue, parents should try to be good role models to their children. When it comes to making people happy, a teenager should realise that making the most important people happy in their lives, is the simple way of living.

Social Life

It is very important to have friends and communication. You should have someone to talk to, it makes you feel better. Meeting people at a church, at the library, at schools, at parties, are good public places to meet people, but don't speak to strangers.

Meeting people through a friend is a good idea, too, now that the Internet, is so widely used there are ways of communication. It is not always safe to be friendly with people you barely know.

A Lesson in Life

There should be two kinds of teachers in life. One who teaches how to make a living, and the other who teaches you how to live. Well, this is to let parents know, that they should spend more time with their children.

Over the years lots has changed, teenagers, now, go out to drink, smoke, take drugs and sleep out as they find that to be their only pleasure. If, parents focused on their children, and try to discipline them from watching too much of television, then a parent and child can have more time together to speak of what is important in life, and the best way to show children how much you care is to spend quality time together.

Teenagers of different cultures behave differently, they are, raised in their own way, by religion and rules. Most changes in a teenagers' life affects them in different ways. Teens need encouragement from their parents, families and friends, in order to be able to learn more about their future, achieving their goals, being positive, trustworthy, honest, and to be able to socialize, and to learn about the facts of life.

Accepting Your Children

Often Parents Don't Accept Their Children

In some cases, children are not accepted in their families for specific reasons like if they have committed a crime or didn't abide by their rule. When parents fail to accept their children.

It Makes You Wonder?

How Does This Happen?

Why Should It Be?

In most cases parents can't come to terms with the issue of the problem. To understand your child, is very important, and, don't listen to other people's opinions, because if you know your child as a parent should, then there should be no doubts about your child.

Forgiving your child should, be easy.
Sometimes a child finds it difficult, to discuss
matters with a parent, and, turns to someone
who advises him/her the wrong way, then this
innocent child, is now into drugs, alcohol,
vandalism and on the streets. It shouldn' be
this way, **if from the start**, parents devoted
their time to their children.

Learning from mistakes, is how life is , and
accepting your child is very important for both
parties, as your child gets older, friendships
develop between parent and child, and, in this
way you stay well together. If a parent, can't
accept their child for a fault, or criminal act,
then it is clear that, this child is not loved
enough, to let go of the incident.

As a result, a child shows no respect, at home,
and parent and child understanding
disappears. If it were **vice verse**, child forgiving
the parent, and asking for acceptance, then, it
would be easy, yet, another **difficult issue**, but
can be solved if child and parent communicate
and understand each other.

It's Your Choice

You Decide What To Do With Your Life

A virus that is killing the continent, it is destroying families, people are dying at an early age, you should avoid this contagious disease. In most parts of the world at least three out of four are infected with HIV a virus that causes AIDS.

It takes just one wrong partner, to get HIV. This is a deadly virus and has no cure. All kinds of people are carrying this disease, the rich, poor, lawyers or doctors, irrespective of race or religion. Don't feel that you know it all, there is still so much more to learn about AIDS.

Issues that put you in a contact with people, infected by this virus are simple thoughts of life. Your friends are at it, you are afraid of what your friends will say if you don't do it. If you are raped or sexually abused. It is difficult to avoid every issue.

You can't say **NO.** A night out with friends and had too much to drink. A trustworthy partner, well, it is what you think. You just couldn't wait to take a chance.

If you think the time is right, you and your partner should have a AIDS test, when you have your test results , then, decide. Even, when using protection, you are not safe.

You either wait for marriage and be safe than having to face problems. Teenagers should be aware of their partner's previous relationships, and make sure that nobody is infected. Innocent ones are infected without their knowledge of this virus. Not many partners will tell you they have HIV.

Stepping Stones

An Opportunity To See More In Life

Just about everything in life is a stepping stone, if you see it this way. An opportunity, to a new job, to getting married, having a new car, to achieve something in life is a stepping stone to a new future. Chances are that it may or may not be possible, but, if you go toward that, then there is a possibility, to get what you want out of life with determination.

Every new attempt, is a stepping stone, to confidence, to create a new effect, or a new experience. Gaining positiveness to achieve your new idea, don't give-up on what you want in life, there is always a way to get to it.

Teach yourself, that to achieve something in life, you have got to be courageous, a good deed, is always treated with a smile.and it will be a successful one, and, if attempted with a simple attitude. To be a selfish person, it would hardly go your way.

Something like this should be shared with loved ones, and, friends. An open-mind about issues is a feeling of hope and not to hold you back from going ahead. When you have a good thing appreciate it, because, when you don't have it, then you will really wish you didn't take it for granted.

You only miss something in life, after you lose it, so try to enjoy what you have, not what can't and will not achieve. A new stepping stone in life is to have, what you can afford, and, not what others think you should. A way for teenagers to be confident.

How To Love

To Learn To Love Someone, Is Accepting Your Partner's Habits

To love someone is not simple, you've got to know your partner and this doesn't happen over-night. You can't love someone, by just spending a few months together, because you will find that your partner is not what you think.

To love your partner unconditionally, one has to grow old together, to know one another well, and, to be soul mates. You discover something new about your partner everyday, as teenagers' experience life, a new point is acknowledged about their partners too.

If you choose to be single, then you will may not know the meaning of love. Love is something that doesn't last for a short or a long period, it could be the kind that is temporary. If you are willing to go further, and, take the chance of staying in a marriage, then you could have true love, which is hard to find.

A kind of love that's in the pit of your tummy, is real love, when only your partner's touch, makes you feel the best. Intimately, you will know for sure. Loving your partner, doesn't necessarily mean, only when you receive gifts, it should be about acceptance, trust, and understanding.

It is to show appreciation, and love one another no matter what. Don't let your partner be embarrassed in public, defend your partner if in a debatable conversation and experience life together.Teenagers need assurance in this way.

A sign of you having no interest in a third party, will tell you that your heart belongs to one person, only. The acceptance of your partner is to be used to the individual's habits, like when getting out of bed in the mornings, coughs, sneezes, common things, like having time out on your own, and, at the end of the day, you are together.

Be apart to do what you enjoy, and feel good to be together again. Any two people, being married, will need time for themselves while the other, is out with friends, and, in this way your relationship becomes a solid one.

As a teenager, you should let your partner know of your plans, some like to marry while as teenage sweethearts, others may prefer to marry when they get older.

Good Manners

Something That Used To Be, And, Seems To Be Forgotten

In the past, manners were taught at home, by our parents, and at school, by our teachers. At a dining table, we used to be polite, and, ask, to be excused, or please pass me the salt.

Now, it seems to be forgotten, or just not, much interest is shown, in being polite to others. This has fallen away, in many households. Lots have changed, the old-fashioned manners, such as please, thank you, when standing in an orderly queue, at a bus station, or when, waiting to be served, and, apologising for bumping into someone, is hardly used.

Children, should be able to understand, that to be polite is very important; if your child is not reminded, then that child will have a poor adult-hood. Something like this should be considered, **always.**

The Cell Phone Trick

When it comes to getting **that** cell phone, it can be your friend or enemy. The initiation, you finally, met someone, you have been waiting for ages, and, you have the number. Being over the first hurdle, is great, but the next stage, is up to you.

When sending your first message, you are basically making the first move, and, setting the mood. Don't get too full on the start, despite the fact you have been constantly day-dreaming, about him keep it casual. If you know a bit about him, it is even better.

The Waiting Game, Your text message, has been carefully crafted. Full-stop, phone-book, find his name, send your message, and, it is out of your hands, as there is nothing you can do, except just wait. In a perfect world, you would get a reply very fast, but, when you don't. **Then you begin to wonder!!!**

What Went Wrong?

Let, one consider the possibilities, an hour or two and no reply, this person is either at a football game, or having dinner with his parents. A day goes by, or has probably run out of a phone card.

You are now not sure what to do. Though, you would want to try once more. If you, have established, that you like each other, then there is nothing, to be embarrassed about, sending a follow-up message, but tread, carefully, you don't want to look desperate.

Best, is to drop the fact, you contacted him before, just ask if he is available to go with you to a concert at the weekend. If, you are again left waiting, then he is just being rude.

Making a date, if he has asked you out first, you have definitely, got one thing straight. He does like you, now you have to write back. It is that tricky mix of alluring unavailability, and, having free time to see him, is what you need to master.

When a guy asks, you, about going out on the weekend, sound like, you are too busy, don't make him think that, you have too much time at hand, especially, when you are free. Decide when you are available, and, what your plans are, and, let him, know. If Cupid, has his way, then you will find the right time to meet.

Mistaken Message

When your phone beeps, you rush to it, and, see his name, but, the message he sent you was meant for someone else. You can **use this** window of opportunity, to get in contact with him. Throw in a casual question, at the end of your message, and, instigate some text banter. You may even find yourselves, chatting for hours, later on. Something teenage girls and boys learn about when with a cell phone.

Judgement on Teenagers

Parents, shouldn't pass judgements on their teenage children, no matter what the situation. A child requires a certain amount of attention from the parent, comments from a parent should be gracious and considerate. Don't belittle your child in the presence of friends or in public, insults should be left alone, this only makes your child feel stupid, and not worthy of you. Don't make silly comments, children can be sensitive, and will be hurt, but, won't show it to you, and will turn the other way.

When what your child learns is basically from the parent, choose how you speak to your child, this is a reflection from you. They grow up with a low self-esteem, and, become isolated, unhappy, and, lonely.

Praise lifts up your child's spirits and a child this way feels positive. A teenager is entitled to their opinions, the willingness to take risks, and have learning experiences on their own. Your child, requires nurturing more than being showed how to do, or attempt a task, this will allow space and the project is a learning process.

Children often are neglected when parents work, allow time for each other it is very important to know your child. If teenagers choose to dress with their choice of clothing, don't be insultiing about it, this is only for that period, a phase that you all have passed or still getting to know more about in this time.

Bullying Teenagers At School

It is a problem that goes on at schools, and not everyone knows it is happening. Teenagers, do experience bullying at school at some point. If you have a busy lifestyle, your child is neglected and not much is noticed at home.

The Important Signs Of Bullying

Loss of belongings, unexplained bruises, a change of route when going to school, not liking to attend school, a change in school activities, if your child comes home with torn clothing, feels sad, lonely, constant tummy aches, a loss of appetite, not having many friends, and the standard of school work is poor. Also, pay attention to cyber bullying, Interent violence towards your teen, is a common issue, with most teens.

Talk to the teacher or principal, even have a discussion with the parent of the child. Change the school or make some improvisation. A child that bullies other children has growing-up issues, and this is inflicted on other children at school, and, often happens for the following reasons :- racial, prejudice, judgemental, which includes, name -calling and insulting.

Activities that your child is not interested in, but, will participate, if forced by a bullying child. Violence is included too. Parents should keep track of their children to avoid these problems.

A Troubled Teen

This happens when parents are divorced, anger, and depression sets in and teenagers become sad. A problem is not seen until suicide is attempted, and, this can be a difficult issue. This is disguised, and not many parents can see it from the start.

Talk to a psychiatrist and keep it confidential, don't discuss with friends or neighbours, because somehow it will be mentioned in public; it is not easy to trust anyone on a subject like this, once in public, your child is affected by gossip, and comments and your child's life is not a secret anymore.

Signs Of Depression In Teenagers

You will notice the change in eating habits, and sleeping patterns are different, the lack of participation in sports activities, consumption of drugs, and alcohol, even smoking becomes a habit, unhappiness, and looking tired. A withdrawal from friends and family; if this is the case don't let your child be alone, make your child feel good by showing love and affection, it will pass. Always tell your teen you love him/her, this is a good feeling for your child, and conversations about daily activities should be discussed too.

Suicidal Teens

People get lonely and become vulnerable. One of the biggest causes of suicide is loneliness, and relationship problems, this can be between married couples, lovers, parents, children or colleagues. Problems can arise because of financial issues, an illness, stress or depression, unemployment, violence in society, crime, rape and molestation.

Another reason is that most children no longer have a proper family life. When teenagers are ignored by parents, they feel lonely. Growing up as teenagers, you need someone trustworthy to talk to.

Talk to someone, in this way suicide can be prevented. At this age all the changes occur. Every year, thousands of school growing youngsters consider suicide, or try to take their own lives.

Rejection, when a person feels rejected by family or friends, it is a difficult situation to deal with. Being Divorced, it affects the family tremendously, children are hurt, and, in most cases have no one to turn to. A lonely and depressed person becomes tired of life, and stops smiling and doesn't care for living anymore. Abuse of alcohol, drugs, neglect, weakness and fear becomes of a depressed person.

Try go to support groups for help, or telephone lifeline for help. It is always good to talk to somebody, make new friends, don't despair. Some issues affect teenagers or others in different ways.

Is Your Teen Lying?

It is not easy to know this, but communication is important to work it out. Treat your teenager with respect, don't panic, try to be calm in situations. Listening to your child, allows you to be a step ahead of the plans your child has. Don't tell your teenager *'don't do it'* - this actually encourages the act. It is up to your child to do what is expected, as this is only an experience. Try not to be harsh in your tone, this will show dominance, and you don't want to do that.

Engage in activities together as a family, this shows a safe and happy family environment, and you will notice that your teenager will be free to speak to you. There shouldn't be barriers for your child in discussing issues.

This will prevent your child from telling lies, and, ideas are shared easily. Trusting your teenager can be difficult, but you only learn from your own mistakes, and, in time trust will be gained, but it won't be easy, and you will move on from that incident.

Parents and teenagers require trust, love, health, communication, understanding, responsibility, respect, self-image, and, discipline, to make their lives acceptable.

Teenagers' Requirements

Teenagers fall into new ideas all the time, they enjoy trying new activities. Hobbies, participating in sports of interest to them, idea of meeting people, trying new diets to stay in in shape, showing responsibility, being friendly, a sign of maturity to form relationships, setting career goals, going shopping, and showing emotions.

So much more to experience and endure, and this is what makes them real people.

Their lives are reflected by their parents, and, in most cases are successful in their careers, because of the useful advice.

In most underprivileged countries, teenagers, form groups and become street gangsters. This happens, often, because, their parents don't have the knowledge of parenting teenagers, and find that to be their way of escaping teenage issues.

This leads to violence, crime, and drugs, with no parental care, teenagers provide for themselves. A sad state but, parents should be informed about their parenting skills, to allow teenagers to be free to explore, and be safe in society. Living In Poverty, doesn't allow you much choice and education is obviously not introduced to the community, and everything goes in different directions without being noticed.

Teenagers In Society

Help your teenager handle pressure at school or at home; show concern in your child's life. A helpful parent should be focused on the requirements of their teenagers. A difficult issue but, it has to be approached at sometime in your lives. Don't deprive your child of the requiremnts, **but make things possible**. To be a healthy teen, an individual has to eat correctly, and make sure health issues are taken care of, have regular examinations to be free of surprise illnesses.

A happy family, has an interest in their children's lives, and have fewer concerns about their teens' behaviour, they will experience minor problems, but nothing to worry about. Living in a safe environment makes it easy connecting with people.

When you are raised in a respected and a good standard community, your friends are not the same, as in other low standard areas. In some cases this works and in others may not.

You shouldn't be under the influence of other children to allow your child to be in a group, but it is up to your child to choose friends, sometimes it can be challenging.

A social life is the idea of being in society, be with people, don't spend too much of time alone.

A teenager, be it a boy or a girl may not be sure of what it is, that interests them. Only, time will tell.

This could be from admitting to being gay, a lesbian, or a transvestite, these are serious issues to look at, but, will be accepted in society, eventually, though friends and family may not find it a pleasant way of living once the word is out, Be by your child's side, don't ignore your teenager just because it feels like an embarrassment to you, and your friends, and that you care about the opinions of others.

At this time you should be thinking of your child's feelings. Your child, shouldn't go through this alone, if you love your child be there, and it is not the decision of the parent at the end of the day.

What Is Your Teenager Thinking?
Will They Be Accepted In Society?
How Will Your Child Be Treated In Public?
Would You Like The Idea?

It doesn't matter about other people, but, when parents put it that way, everything falls apart in a family.

To know your teenager, think about you, in your time, it was different, but, now work together. Parents can learn more from teenagers in the times of today, and think about what they have missed, and, could still experience this together.

A good way of learning with your teenage children.

When you make decisions, teenagers want to do the same, but, on what they feel is good for them.
Life is full of surprises, you could have anything you want in life, only if you put your mind to it, don't give up on life, with positive thinking, you can make possibilities come true.

Juvenile Delinquency

Juveniles Are Out Of Control In Our Society

If you are still a virgin as a teenager, then you must be proud of it. You should treasure yourself, have enough dignity, pride and self-worth, to make informed decisions your are comfortable with, not to keep the tension of a totally selfish person. There is more to life than just sex, with one night stands, and, taking responsibility for your actions, is not often that way.

To be respected and accepted in society, you have to make this possible. Don't get involved with people that just feel, that, they can get what they want, unfortunately, society is riddled with youngsters that don't take responsibility for their actions.

Vandalism

This is one of the biggest act of violence, writing on clean painted walls, damaging dustbins, littering, breaking of school property, and, defacing any property. The problem arises when children are abandoned, or neglected.

Living in a society with low standards, people tend to have a low self-esteem in situations like this. Groups are formed, and, plans are made to abuse other people. Stealing becomes another practice for those who can't afford to buy a specific item. This, actually turns out to be a daily routine.

Innocent people get attacked, because these gangs become violent, and, streets are not safe any more, in the day time or at night. In most cases gangs have leaders, that control the daily tasks.

This, in most cases, is how children grow up to be, juveniles who are out of control especially, when there is no adult supervision. To prevent this from happening, there should be other interests to get these gangs off the streets. Something to look forward to as a career, social workers should allow for legal adoption and a family is formed and habits are changed. Create music classes, this will distract their minds from being destructive. Some teenager don't have the ability of setting goals.

Remember that everything you achieve in life takes time, the quality of you, should be of high regard and always, heads up, and shoulders upright, to look good at any place you go. With confidence and talking to people, allows you go one step further.

Teenagers have different attitudes in life, they are often faced with decisions, and, if they come from a background with single parents, then their future is not often a stable one. This happens when one parent has full responsibility, of a teenager. Attitudes change when children spend all their time with only their friends, and, barely see their parents.

They tend to live separate lives, and, this causes many problems for teenagers and parents. Issues like this happens in many cases, and in most cases, the reason for street children and gangsters.

Children, that live the same kind of life get together and live as they wish. They grow into disrespectful and disreputable children, and fail to comply with any chore at home,and, lose interest of listening to their parent in any way. If teenagers are responsible, on their own, they are capable of managing tasks.

As a single parent or a couple, parents must realise, that nothing in a teenager's life should be taken for granted. Learn to love and appreciate each other, is a way to learn more about raising teenagers.

Parent Education

You become a parent with anticipation and excitement. Parent education is very important, and special programmes can be taken to avoid the neglect of children and child abuse. Successful parent education helps parents to acquire parenting and problem-solving skills.

This helps to have a healthy family and to prevent children from being aggressive, or disrespectful to each other. When parents fail to understand their children's behaviour and therefore a change of attitude follows the issue.

Both parents must protect their children, and attend parent educating classes to learn from new experiences, or information; it helps parents to be educated, to teach their children, new skills and know differently of how to discipline their children at home, to let their lives as teenagers be free and exciting.

Parent education is for parents who lack the knowledge, of how to raise their teenagers. Parenthood can be difficult, but, with special training, they can learn more.

Relationships

Relationships Should Go Hand In
Hand

Argumentative Relationships

Teenagers Should Know Of Such
Issues

An issue that can be monotonous, and won't
stop until someone lets go. This could be
caused, by jealousy, when one partner doesn't
like the other interacting with others, being
disorganised in your schedules, not spending
time together, or just being moody.

The blame falls on the other person. When
teenagers argue, it is normally about the same
issue, a problem, that needs to be fixed. To
avoid arguments, talk sensibly, the excuse of
your being too busy should be excluded. You
become tearful, angry, you lose control,
because, you are not reasoning with your
partner about your problem.

This makes you manipulative, as you go along. You start feeling sorry for yourself, when you know that, you don't want to do anything about your agrumentative habits. It could be changed, but time is required.

Share the daily plan, for each day, if you are not ready for a commitment let your partner know about it. When you can't stop arguing , you lose respect ,and care for each other, and, you slip away from the relationship.

YOU

To Let People Know That Just Being YOU Is Important. Try To Be Yourself Rather Than Wish You Were Someone Else.

I was often told to be a positive person, and never bother about other people's opinions, just be yourself. Well, that is true, why should you think of what others 'say' when, you can do whatever you feel like. Just do what you feel is right.

Do not let yourself go to the point that you will be feeling sorry for yourself.
Life shouldn't be that way. Life is what we make of it, it is not up to the other person, it is 'you' that has to make a change in your life.

How Does One Live?

Being just 'you' is important, try not to be obsessed with pleasures in life. Allow time for yourself, in this way you can enjoy your day, and, the time with your loved ones.
Make sure to get enough sleep, keep fit. Eat healthy foods. The life of living like a celebrity is a weak thought, it just makes you a different person.

Going to the doctors continuously for every little ache that you have is just for hypochondriacs. Those are people, who always worry about their health, and are never cured of their illnesses.

It is exciting when something good happens, but this only happens when you expect a good deed to come along, not when you become obsessional about it.

To live your life as you want, it is important, and, to be free is a great feeling too.
Having to live in a safe environment, being happy, you should be good in health, to be in love and have a family.

You should be financially secure, and, have a social life. Be you, someone with achievement, never be scared of taking risks in life. You can only achieve your goals when you put your mind to it.

Occasional drinks with family and friends allows you to enjoy the moment better and feel good about yourself.

What Do You Want From Life?

Everyone wants to have what other people have.

How Can Anyone Even Think Like That?

People should focus on their requirements.
Purchase, what is really needed, you save
much more.
An individual should be thinking of living a
simple and affordable way.

Try to be friendly with the people around you,
enjoy life, forgive those who have said and
done anything to you in the past.

Life is too short to show anger toward anyone
close to you. Let there be love between you,
not hatred, it is what life is all about. Give
yourself a chance to work out what is important
to you, and there will be appreciation toward
what is required.

Having a life, is a good start, try not to wait, on
living your life, treat each day as a new one, a
new beginning, it gives you more chances of
being happy, and, achieving what is aimed for.
Having to be a wealthy person is not all, most
important is to be an educated one, and enjoy
what you have.

Happiness comes with laughter, there will be sadness, of course, but we are faced with all kinds of traumatic experiences. Wounds don't heal, it always re-opens, but with life you got to go forward. Have time for yourself, enjoy your life to the fullest.

Spoil yourself once in a while by going out with friends, it makes you look forward to the event and having fun by meeting new people.

ACCEPTANCE

First you accept yourself. Accepting compliments, when someone tells you, that the dress you wearing, looks lovely on you, you accept the compliment. That must be a true compliment. If you are told that your cooking is great, and you know, for a fact, that it is not true, then the person is just trying to be polite. To accept a compliment, you must be true to yourself.

A person that accepts a compliment whole-heartedly, is someone who is not afraid to take risks, is lucky, and, confident.

Try something embarrassing, like, karaoke, maybe, this will cheer you up, and be confident. Do things, that you have been putting off for a while, you will, learn to accept yourself. Take a risk, it may not be as scary as you thought. If you believe you are great, everybody else will think you are too. Challenge, any obstacle, this will make you feel good.

Teenagers live and learn.

Hobbies

To Have Something To Do At Any Age

Some people, have hobbies and some don't. When a person feels, like doing something different, there are many choices when it comes to having a hobby. It is very important to be occupied with an interesting activity, this allows your mind to be stress-free.

There are choices, like collecting rare books, antiques, like brass ware, copper, silver, or the interest in stamps, charms, stickers of different kinds, from all different countries. Flags of the world, stone searching, trying to find stones of different shapes, or sizes, big or small, badges with unique colours or phrases, kinds of pens, cars, vintage or new, kinds of hats for all kinds of people, shells, from your visits to beaches, coins or notes in money, from the oldest to the newest, and maybe even beer mugs.

Old lanterns, can be interesting too. Make your hobby interesting, one can cut out pictures to make a picture book, but with unusual pictures. Get a camera, take photos of the beautiful sites our world has to offer, and, make it a pleasurable one. You will enjoy it better than charging a fee for photos. Collectables like, miniature, ships, aircrafts, or plant trees that are different, like the bonzai tree.

A hobby is for someone that can take time-out to relax, and enjoy something from a stressful day at school or work.

Getting Along With Your Parents

It can be a difficult process to get on with parents, especially, if they don't have the understanding, and only see issues from one point of view. If they have more than one child, parents tend to have a favourite.

Issues like when your parents want for you what they couldn't achieve, when they were as teens, you can only be what you want to. If you have problems getting along with your parents, make a note of what upsets, or gets them angry, and what you are afraid of when in conversation, you should compromise about these problems during a meal, and discuss these points in a pleasant manner.

If there are changes, it will be made and coversation will be easier. Parents should treat their children equally, your child can be loved differently but don't neglect the other, because if you have a special one, this won't be good for a child's mental stability.

Be Together

When in a relationship, one doesn't realise, the effort made to have this special life together. As a person in love, there are many important things in life, that needs to be taken into consideration. The fact that you have a relationship, doesn't necessarily mean, you have it all.

Time, and effort, to be with your partner, and to do normal stuff, go out together, make time for each other, don't spend your valuable time out with friends, and neglect the relationship, especially, if you know, that it is going good. Make time for your friends, and enjoy what you have, show your partner, you are trustworthy, make an effort to be together, no matter what.

Go away together, on a special celebration, don't carry your cell phone, when you are together, keep business deals out of the way, when you are in a public place, be relaxed, enjoy the day, and make your partner laugh about something, talk about good times ,and bad ones, understand each other, and communicate if there is a problem. To love and know your partner.

Try not to put pressure on each other about little issues. Allow yourselves to be free, and, loving. Be together, and you will feel that you can go a long way. If you love your partner, there can be no obstacle, in your way. Get to know your partner's habits and connect equally.

Connecting to family and friends is a great way to experience life for teenagers.

Raising Teenagers is challenging, communication is the key to all relationships don't ignore this important factor of life.

Spending time with your child from day one will allow you to be friends and understand each other better.

Many issues are solved only because you didn't neglect the most important years of your child and that starts from the infancy age.

As a result this educational information should enlighten your mind and thoughts about raising teenagers.

Special Thanks: To Gary and Sandra for taking time in the proof reading.

About the author

I am South African, of Indian decent, now living in the most Southern part of Croatia. A new beginning and enjoying every moment of it.